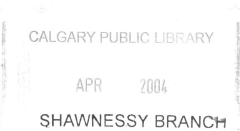

The Story of Flight
AIR COMBAT

Crabtree Publishing Company
www.crabtreebooks.com

PMB 16A, 350 Fifth Avenue,
Suite 3308
New York, NY 10118

612 Welland Avenue
St. Catharines, Ontario
L2M 5V6

Published in 2004 by
Crabtree Publishing Company

Coordinating editor: Ellen Rodger
Project editors: Sean Charlebois, Carrie Gleason
Production coordinator: Rose Gowsell

Created and Produced by
David West Children's Books

Project Development, Design, and Concept
David West Children's Books:
Designer: Rob Shone
Editor: Gail Bushnell
Illustrators: James Field, Mike Lacey & Stephen Sweet
(SGA), Gary Slater & Steve Weston (Specs Art), Iole Rosa
(Allied Artists), Alain Salesse (Contact Jupiter), Alex
Pang
Picture Research: Carlotta Cooper

Photo Credits:
Abbreviations: t-top, m-middle, b-bottom, r-right,
l-left, c-center.

Front cover & pages 7, 10t, 18t & b - The Flight
Collection. 4, 24, 25, 28b - BAE Systems. 5, 9, 10b,
12b, 14t, 16t & b - The Culture Archive. 6, 8, 12t,
14b - Royal Air Force Museum. 21, 28t - NASA.

06 05 04 03

10 9 8 7 6 5 4 3 2 1

Library of Congress Cataloging-in-Publication Data
Hansen, Ole Steen.
    Air combat/ written by Ole Steen Hansen.
        p. cm. -- (The story of flight)
Includes index.
Summary: Describes the tactics of air combat, famous flying aces,
and the fighter planes that were used in World Wars I and II, the
Korean War, the Cold War, Vietnam, and the Gulf War.
ISBN 0-7787-1206-0 (RLB : alk. paper) -- ISBN 0-7787-1222-2 (PB :
alk. paper)
    1. Air warfare--Juvenile literature. [1. Air warfare. 2. Aeronautics,
Military.] I. Title.
II. Series.
    UG630.H37 2003
    358.4'3--dc22
                                                                    2003016000

The Story of Flight

AIR COMBAT

Ole Steen Hansen

Crabtree Publishing Company
www.crabtreebooks.com

CONTENTS

MODERN FIGHTER DESIGN
Today's fighters, such as the F-16, are very advanced, but they still have similarities to their World War I ancestors. Their weapons point forward, they are fast, maneuverable, and require an expert pilot to fly in air combat situations.

INTRODUCTION

Fighters have always been the fastest and most maneuverable military aircraft. Their pilots need to be aggressive and quick thinking. Since the beginning of air wars, fighters have been used to attack enemy aircraft, win air superiority, and dominate the sky. Today, fighters are mainly used to shoot down observation planes and bombers.

SPAD XII
The World War I SPAD fighter was a fast plane for its time. It was armed with two forward-firing machine-guns.

LOCKHEED P-38 LIGHTNING
The first aircraft destroyed by the American P-38 fighter during World War II was a German FW-200 observation and bomber aircraft shot down near Iceland.

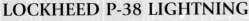

THE DEADLY SKIES

Air combat started during World War I (1914–18), when both sides wanted to destroy enemy planes that observed troops. Soon, fighters flew with the sole aim of shooting down the enemy.

VOISIN 3

French pilots Joseph Frantz and Louis Quénault won the first air combat victory ever in a Voisin. They shot down a German observation plane on October 5, 1914.

During World War I, artillery guns killed the most people, but the big guns could only hit enemy **trenches** if they knew where they were. Observers in balloons and observation aircraft spotted the enemy. They also told the gunners down below whether the guns had hit their targets, which made even unarmed observation planes dangerous.

BURSTING BALLOONS

Fighter planes, like this Farman Shorthorn, were used to shoot down enemy observers and their balloons. It was a dangerous job because the balloons were often well defended.

PUSHER PLANE TACTICS

On some pusher planes the gunner in front could swing his gun. This gave the pusher an arc of fire in front. It had a blind spot in the rear, as most fighters do, but by flying in a circle formation they could protect each other's tails. This prevented enemy attacks from behind.

Shooting them down with rifles or pistols was very difficult. Machine-guns made it easier, but firing a gun from an aircraft required skill and balance. The machine-guns needed to be fixed to the aircraft so the pilot could fly and aim at the same time. This was the birth of the fighter aircraft. Some early fighters had the engine mounted in the back, but soon systems were invented that allowed machine-guns to fire between the rotating propeller blades without hitting them.

Pilot Training

During World War I, pilot training consisted of little more than learning to fly the aircraft without crashing it when landing back at the airfield. Here, trainee pilots are learning in a Farman Shorthorn. New pilots suffered heavy losses at the **front** when they met more experienced enemy pilots who could fly their fighters through all kinds of maneuvers.

DOGFIGHT

WERNER VOSS

Werner Voss joined the German cavalry during World War I. In 1915 he transferred to the Air Force and became one of the best German fighter pilots, with 48 victories to his credit. He was 20 years old when he was killed.

Fighters soon began attacking each other. A fight in which an enemy aircraft turned around again and again was called a dogfight. The most famous dogfight of World War I took place on September 23, 1917.

Late in the afternoon, British fighters were out protecting their observation planes and looking for German aircraft. Six very experienced British pilots flying SE5s suddenly saw a lone German Fokker Triplane attacking an SE5 down below. Soon, the SE5s were attacking the Fokker, which was flown by expert pilot Werner Voss. For ten long minutes Voss fought the SE5s.

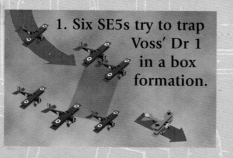

VOSS' TACTICS

Voss was outnumbered by the SE5s, but he turned toward them and faced their attack. A basic rule of air combat is to ensure the enemy does not get on your tail. It is also important to only fire at short range and to keep an eye on your enemy at all times.

1. Six SE5s try to trap Voss' Dr 1 in a box formation.

2. Voss spins his triplane around and attacks.

Parachutes

Although parachutes had been invented, only observation balloonists were allowed to use them during World War I. Generals believed pilots would jump from their airplanes before they entered combat if they wore parachutes.

According to one British pilot "his flying was wonderful, his courage magnificent… he is the bravest German airman whom it has been my privilege to fight." Voss managed to damage all the British planes, but nineteen-year-old Rhys Davis killed him with a short range burst of fire. Rhys Davis himself was shot down two months later, only a short distance from where Voss was killed.

A NERVE-RACKING EXPERIENCE

A British pilot whose SE5 was damaged by Voss remembered getting out of his aircraft back at the airfield: "I practically collapsed. For a minute or two everything went black. It seemed pitch dark and I could hear someone asking where I had been hit. I wanted to laugh because I had managed to get down without crashing, but instead I started to cry."

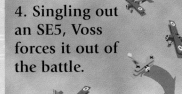

3. Flying through the SE5 formation he turns again and attacks from behind.

4. Singling out an SE5, Voss forces it out of the battle.

5. Again and again the Dr 1 turns to face its attackers.

PEACETIME

During the 20 years between the World Wars (1919–39), the speed of fighters went up from 143 mph (230 km/h) to 360 mph (580 km/h). More aircraft were developed in wartime than during peacetime.

World War I had been terrible. People called it "the war to end all wars." Very few new fighter planes were developed in the two decades that followed.

SIR HUGH TRENCHARD

For most of World War I, the British Army and Royal Navy operated their own air forces. In mid-1918 they were joined to form the Royal Air Force (RAF). After the war the military chiefs tried to go back to the earlier system. Sir Hugh Trenchard prevented this and the RAF became a model for countries throughout the world.

POLIKARPOV I-16
Country: Soviet Union
Length: 19 ft 7 in (5.9 m)
Wingspan: 29 ft 6 in (9 m)
Speed: 242 mph (389 km/h)
First flown: December 1933

Sinking the Ostfriesland

In 1921, British flyer, William "Billy" Mitchell used a formation of airplanes to sink a German battleship captured during World War I. With this target practice, Mitchell proved that aircraft could sink warships. During World War II bombers and fighters flying from aircraft carriers dominated the war at sea.

GLOSTER GLADIATOR
Country: Great Britain
Length: 27 ft 5 in (8.3 m)
Wingspan: 32 ft 3 in (9.8 m)
Speed: 215 mph (346 km/h)
First flown: September 1934

Then it became apparent there would be another war, and some countries started to design new fighters. The age of the open cockpit biplane was nearing its end by the 1930s. Some of the 1930s fighters seen here are still biplanes and some have **retractable** landing gear. The I-16 has an open cockpit, although it was the first fighter to have both retractable landing gear and a cantilever monoplane wing not supported by struts and wires. The Gloster Gladiator was the first Royal Air Force fighter with an enclosed cockpit. Pilots sometimes left it open because they liked to feel the wind on their skin.

GRUMMAN F3F
Country: USA
Length: 23 ft (7 m)
Wingspan: 32 ft (9.7 m)
Speed: 239 mph (384 km/h)
First flown: March 1935

FOKKER DXXI
Country: Netherlands
Length: 26 ft 10 in (8.2 m)
Wingspan: 36 ft 1 in (11 m)
Speed: 286 mph (460 km/h)
First flown: February 1936

THE MARTIN B-10
The Martin B-10 was the most modern bomber of its day when ordered in 1933 by the U.S. Army Air Corps. This monoplane was as fast or faster than most fighters, which were still biplanes. The B-10 gunner sat inside the turret. Since the bombs were stowed inside and the wheels were retractable, the B-10 had a streamlined shape and could go faster.

BATTLE OVER ENGLAND

When World War II started in 1939, the German army quickly conquered many countries in Europe. Through the summer and autumn of 1940, they were stopped for the first time in the Battle of Britain.

The battle was the first in history to be fought completely in the air. The Germans were trying to destroy Britain's Royal Air Force (RAF).

AIRFIELDS
Many of the grass-covered airfields used by the RAF were targeted and bombed by the Germans during the Battle of Britain. British pilots were also outnumbered in the air, but they won the battle anyway.

Cramped Cockpits
A fighter cockpit was cramped and packed with instruments and controls. It was noisy, especially when climbing at full throttle. Flying at high speeds, the fighters had only seconds to hit the enemy with one of their eight machine-guns.

They hoped to destroy the British navy and invade Britain. Battling in the air at high speed was a strange and nerve-racking experience. A Spitfire pilot would climb to face the enemy with his squadron. The enemy closed in great numbers, sometimes eight Spitfires to 100 or more enemy fighters and bombers. Whoever saw the opponent first would place his squadron in a good attacking position. The combat lasted only minutes, with aircraft filling the sky, and it was extremely difficult to watch everything going on. Suddenly the sky would seem empty as the planes quickly flew far away from the scene. It was very dangerous, but with luck and skill some pilots managed to survive.

BANDITS AT SIX O'CLOCK

Airmen used the clock code to describe over the radio where allies, enemies, and targets were located in relation to their own aircraft. "Bandits at six o'clock high" meant "enemy aircraft right behind and above you." A target "at two o'clock" was in front of your aircraft to the right. The code is still used in air combat today.

RAGING SKIES

Fighters lose speed or altitude when turning hard. Sometimes fighters ended up chasing each other low over the English landscape.

NIGHT FIGHTER

At the beginning of World War II bombers suffered heavy losses from fighter attacks. Bombers defended themselves with machine-guns, but were still shot down. The Royal Air Force Bomber Command decided it would be better to bomb at night.

Radar image

Map showing coastline

NIGHT VISION
Pilots wore night goggles to adjust their sight to night conditions before taking off. Such goggles were also used to test a pilot's night vision.

At first, fighters had difficulty finding the bombers at night. The bombers also had great problems finding their targets at night, but over the years electronic equipment and **radar** were fitted in bombers as well as fighters. Some devices helped the aircraft to "see" in the night and find their targets, while others tried to jam, or block, the enemy radar. The aerial night battles became deadly electronic hide and seek games. There were no great dogfights at night because few aircraft were close enough to see each other in the dark. Most night combat involved lone, heavily armed night fighters hunting among the hundreds of bombers that tried to remain unseen. The bomber's greatest chance of survival was to remain unseen or to spot the fighter with enough time to disappear quickly, either by maneuvering wildly or by flying into clouds.

Black Widow
Night fighters were much heavier and less maneuverable than the single-engined day fighters. Night fighters had to carry radar equipment to help them find the bombers and sneak in unseen for the kill. The American Northrop P-61 Black Widow was the largest night fighter of World War II. It was also the first to be designed purely for fighting at night.

RADAR

An important type of airborne radar was the British H2S. It was contained in a bubble under the bomber. The navigator could see an image of the land beneath the aircraft on a screen. The image often looked confusing, but coastlines could be seen clearly. The H2S helped British bomber crews find German cities near the coast. A city with a large lake nearby could also be identified.

A SHOT IN THE DARK

German night fighters like this Messerschmitt Bf 110 often aimed at an enemy's wings. The wings of a bomber contained a lot of fuel and burned easily. Fire spread quickly and often very few of the crew managed to escape by parachute.

PROP VERSES JET

ADOLF GALLAND

German ace pilot, Adolf Galland shot down a total of 104 Allied **aircraft** during World War II. He shot down 7 of these while flying an Me 262 in the last months of the war.

The jet engine was invented before World War II, but the first jets were only developed during the war. Toward the end of World War II, jets fought propeller driven aircraft. Most fighter jets at this time were German.

Jet powered fighters soon proved superior in air combat. The propeller driven fighters could make tighter turns, but jets were faster. A jet pilot could decide whether to fight or fly away to get in a better position before attacking. The German twin jet-engined Messerschmitt Me 262 was regarded by many as the best fighter of the war. Yet the Me 262s still suffered many losses. The jets burned their fuel rapidly and could not stay in the air long.

Korean Air Battles

During the **Korean War** (1950–53), jet fighters fought each other for the first time, but there were still some piston engined aircraft in service. This meant that jets and propeller driven aircraft also fought each other. The American F-82 Twin Mustang, seen here with radar for night fighting under the wing, was used a lot early in the war. Its long range was an important asset.

16

Their engines had a life of only about 25 hours running time. Engines required careful handling because they would "flame out," or stop, in the air or even burn out. Besides, Allied bombing had almost stopped German fuel production, so there was not enough to keep all the jets in the air, much less to train the pilots to fly them.

HEINKEL HE 162 "SALAMANDER"

The He 162 was designed, built, and test flown in just 90 days. It was partly made of wood and proved very difficult to fly. Nine pilots were killed in accidents. Only one He 162 ever claimed to have shot down an Allied fighter.

DOWN TO EARTH

When landing and taking off, the Me 262s were very vulnerable to attacks from American Mustangs. On October 7, 1944, Lt. Urban L. Drew shot down two Me 262s as they took off.

COLD WAR STAND-OFF

The Cold War started in 1945 immediately after World War II ended. During the war, the world's superpowers, the United States and the Soviet Union, both feared the other would attack with nuclear weapons.

CONVAIR B-58 HUSTLER
The fastest of the early nuclear bombers was the B-58 flyer, which flew at twice the speed of sound. It was very expensive and only had a short service life.

Tupolev TU-22M "Backfire"
Around 300 TU-22M "Backfires" were built before production ended in 1993. The first flight was in 1969. The "Backfire" has swing wings and is capable of flying at Mach 2, or twice the speed of sound, at high altitude. In the denser atmosphere lower to the ground it can reach almost the speed of sound. A single "Backfire" could destroy a number of cities with its load of nuclear bombs or cruise missiles. Since a third World War never broke out, the "Backfire," like other Cold War bombers, was never used for a nuclear strike.

AIR BURST
In July 1957 a F-89J Scorpion from the U.S. Air Force test fired a Genie nuclear air-to-air missile for the first time. The rocket exploded high in the sky, and the fighter had to turn quickly to avoid being destroyed by the blast of its own missile!

RIVALS

The Cold War bomber destroyers included three types. The F-102 was the first American **supersonic** all-weather jet interceptor. The fire control system fired its rockets and missiles automatically at the right moment. The MiG-25 was designed to fly at three times the speed of sound to intercept the American bombers! The Canadian CF-100 was intended mainly to destroy Soviet bombers flying over the North Pole to attack North America.

Convair F-102
Delta Dagger

Mikoyan/Gurevich
MiG-25 "Foxbat"

Avro Canada
CF-100 "Canuck"

During World War II, it usually took hundreds of bombers to damage a city. Ten years later, a single bomber carrying nuclear weapons could completely destroy several big cities. The new bombers were faster and **interceptor** fighters had to be able to fly just as fast to stop bombers long before they reached their target. Many fighters of the 1950s and 1960s were not designed to engage in dogfights and shoot down other fighters. They were meant to destroy bombers. In the United States, some fighters were even armed with nuclear air-to-air weapons. The Genie was a rocket, while the Falcon was a guided missile. The blast from these weapons could destroy bombers, even if they exploded a great distance away from the incoming plane.

19

ROLLING THUNDER

In the late 1950s, it was thought that technology in the form of fast fighters, long range bombers, and more accurate missiles had replaced traditional air combat. The Vietnam War in the 1960s proved that technology could not replace the skills of a good pilot.

The ground war in Vietnam from the early 1960s to 1975 was fought mainly in South Vietnam. There were also fierce air battles over North Vietnam. In campaigns such as "Rolling Thunder" (1965–68) and "Linebacker" (1972) the U.S. Air Force tried to stop the North Vietnamese **communists** from supporting the war in the south.

ROBIN OLDS

Robin Olds fought in both World War II and Vietnam. The U.S. Air Force did not do dogfight training after the Korean War ended (1953). In Vietnam, experts such as Robin Olds taught young pilots how to fly in old-style air combat.

HEAT SEEKERS

The Sidewinder heat seeking missile was often used in Vietnam, but only one in ten air-to-air missiles hit their target. The most common way of avoiding a missile was to turn hard at the last possible moment. The missile would try to follow, but it could not turn as hard as the aircraft, so it would streak past and soon run out of fuel.

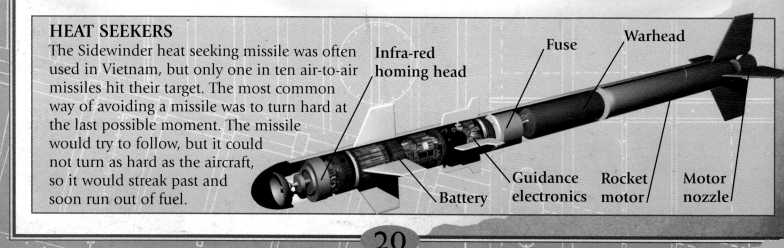

Infra-red homing head · Fuse · Warhead · Battery · Guidance electronics · Rocket motor · Motor nozzle

American bombers, such as the F-105 Thunderchief, were escorted by fighters such as the F-4 Phantom. The Americans fought under rules of engagement that dictated that they should identify the enemy fighters first. Due to the high speeds they often ended up flying so close that they could not use their missiles! The jets were dogfighting in the air as fighters had always done.

NEAR MISS

Often, American aircraft met masses of anti-aircraft missiles instead of North Vietnamese fighters. Here a couple of F-4 Phantoms flying from U.S. Navy aircraft carriers maneuver to avoid a North Vietnamese surface-to-air missile (SAM) fired from the ground.

Bombing Run

The "Rolling Thunder" campaign, carried out by planes such as the F-105 Thunderchief (left), was fought under rules that made it difficult for the U.S. Air Force to wipe out the North Vietnamese defenses. Targets and weapons were selected in Washington, thousands of miles from the aerial battlefield. Hanoi, the capital of North Vietnam, and the fighter airfields around it, were off-limits for a long time. This made it easier for the North Vietnamese to organize their defenses.

"WING MEN"

The basic fighter team is made up of a pilot looking for the enemy and a "wing man" to watch its tail. The two person team may be doubled to make a formation of four aircraft.

MANEUVERS

There is no guarantee that a missile will hit an enemy, so fighters still have to maneuver to position themselves for an attack. Today's fighter pilots need to know what to do if they find an enemy on their tail, just like pilots in World War I and World War II did.

The Break:
Do not try to run! A defender breaking hard into the direction of an attacker becomes a more difficult target to hit.

Attacker

Defender

High Speed Yo-Yo: Climb hard. This slows the defender down and the pilot can now dive on the attacker who suddenly has an aircraft on his own tail!

Defender

Attacker

Sitting in a
simulator you
almost feel like
you are really
flying. Pilots use
simulators to train
for situations that
are too dangerous
to practice.

TOP GUN

The early air battles of the Vietnam War showed that American pilots did not do as well in air combat as expected. They relied too much on technology.

In 1969, the U.S. Navy set up their Top Gun school. Fighter pilots were taught air combat under simulated, but very realistic, conditions. Top Gun students fly against different kinds of fighters to learn how to use their own skills to the best advantage. Top Gun instructors use tactics that enemies are expected to use. In 1972, one Top Gun graduate, Randy Cunningham, flying a F-4 Phantom with radar operator Willie Driscoll in the rear seat, shot down three North Vietnamese fighters during one flight. Their own aircraft was damaged and they had to eject over the sea on their way back to the aircraft carrier. They were later picked up by a helicopter.

Viffing
The Harrier can take-off and land vertically by pointing its jet nozzles downward. By pointing them slightly forward, or "Viffing" they can brake hard in the air, making an enemy overshoot. During the **Falklands War** in 1982, British Sea Harriers shot down many Argentine aircraft while losing none of their own in air combat.

Defender

The Scissors:
Here the defender tries to roll himself into position behind the attacker, but the attacker also rolls. The most maneuverable fighter will win in a situation like this.

High G Barrel Roll:
By maneuvering hard the defender makes himself a difficult target and slows down. The attacker overshoots and becomes the target.

Attacker

Attacker

Defender

NEW IDEAS

During the 1970s, Western nations saw a need for a small, highly maneuverable fighter. It would be deployed in larger numbers, so it had to be cheaper than the big fighters.

This new fighter became the F-16 Fighting Falcon. The F-16 has a powerful engine that makes it possible to climb while turning hard, a maneuver that would cause an older jet, such as the Phantom, to lose altitude. The F-16 was designed to be wildly unstable. In fact, 100 small corrections per second were needed with the controls just to keep it on the right track.

ELECTRONIC COUNTER MEASURES
Radar is used both to detect a fighter and to control missiles. Modern fighters have radar warning receivers to tell the pilot they are being tracked. They also have jammers to disrupt enemy radar.

Hydraulic systems

Side-stick controller

Servo actuators

Avionics

COMPUTER PILOTS
When the F-16 pilot touches the side-stick controller, information is sent to a computer. The computer decides how to move controls such as the elevators, ailerons, flaps, and rudder in order to execute the maneuver most efficiently. The computer also prevents the plane from exceeding certain limits so the pilot can keep a better eye on the enemy.

No pilot can do that, but a computer can, and the F-16 is controlled by a computer. The pilot does not feel how unstable the plane is, but if the aircraft is asked to turn hard it will immediately do so, since its instability makes it want to turn rather than fly straight and level.

FIRE AND FORGET
New radar controlled missiles home in on a target without the fighter having to direct it by using its own radar.

SAAB 39 Gripen
The F-16 was developed as a combined fighter and bomber. The Swedish SAAB 39 Gripen, first flown in 1988, fourteen years after the F-16, is also a highly maneuverable fighter that can carry a bomb load. This makes it economical for air forces because they get two for one!

TODAY'S COMBAT AIRCRAFT

Today's fighters can shoot down an enemy beyond visual range using radar and radar controlled missiles. They must also be prepared to fight it out at close range like fighter pilots have always done.

The Su-35 has remarkable maneuverability and carries many missiles. The Su-35 is a first class dogfighter, but it is also a multi-role fighter that flies as a bomber. The latest European combat aircraft, the Eurofighter Typhoon, is also a multi-role fighter aircraft.

AT THE CONTROLS
Many instruments, computers, radar, and digital displays help today's fighter pilots fly the aircraft, select weapons, and keep an eye on the enemy, as seen in the Eurofighter cockpit illustration above.

EUROFIGHTER TYPHOON
Country: Britain, Germany, Italy, and Spain
Length: 52 ft 4 in (15.9 m)
Wingspan: 35 ft 11 in (11 m)
Speed: 1,280 mph (2,060 km/h)

SU-35
Country: Russia
Length: 72 ft 9 in (22.2 m)
Wingspan: 49 ft 9 in (15.2 m)
Speed: 1,553 mph (2,500 km/h)

MUNITIONS

Modern multi-role fighters can be equipped with a large variety of missiles that make it possible to destroy different kinds of targets. This ammunition is very expensive, but essential in destroying military targets only. This means that fewer civilians are killed in military accidents.

Top to bottom: Sidewinder, anti-ship missile, anti-runway missile, retarded bomb, air-to-ground missile, "smart" bomb.

LOCKHEED BOEING F-22 RAPTOR

Country: USA
Length: 62 ft 8 in (18.9 m)
Wingspan: 44 ft 6 in (13.6 m)
Speed: 1,088 mph (1,750 km/h)

Throughout the history of air combat, the majority of fighters that were shot down were taken by surprise and never saw their enemy. With beyond-visual-range missiles, this threat is becoming even greater. The F-117 stealth bomber does not show up on radar and cannot be shot down with these missiles. Technology from the F-117 was used in the design of the F-22 fighter, which is also difficult to see on radar.

LOCKHEED F-117A

Country: USA
Length: 65 ft 11 in (20.1 m)
Wingspan: 43 ft 4 in (13.2 m)
Speed: 700 mph (1,125 km/h)

Ground Attack

The A-10 is a highly maneuverable ground attack aircraft originally designed for destroying tanks. In combat, A-10s usually carry some Sidewinder heat seeking missiles to defend themselves against enemy fighters. Their main focus is to concentrate on attacking ground targets, so like most bombers, they try to stay away from air combat.

FUTURE FIGHTERS

Fighters without pilots, fighters that heal themselves if hit by bullets, and spy planes shaped like insects are just some of the fantastic combat aircraft designs planned for the future.

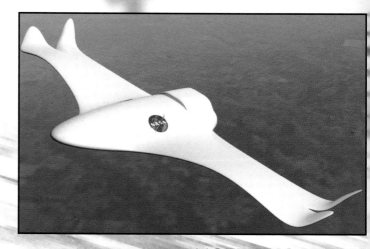

MORPHING PLANES
In the United States, NASA researches morphing planes that can change shape in the air. NASA predicts that it will be at least 20 years before these planes will be ready to fly.

Future Weapons
During the World Wars companies competed with each other to sell military aircraft. Today it has become so expensive to develop new fighters that very few companies in the world have the resources to do it. There will be few competitors to the Lockheed Martin F-35, which will come in a number of versions to replace the F-16 and other combat aircraft.

Unmanned aircraft are already in use and occasionally they have been armed. With no pilot's life to risk, an unmanned aircraft, whether it is a spy plane, a fighter, or a bomber, can do more dangerous maneuvers. The aircraft can be controlled from the ground or from Airborne Warning and Control System (AWACS) radar planes flying and monitoring the battle.

NEW SHAPES

Today's unmanned aircraft are used mostly for observation, but Northrop Grumman is working on this dedicated unmanned combat aircraft for the U.S. Navy. Other types are also under development.

In the United States, the National Aeronautics and Space Administration (NASA) is studying new metals and materials for aircraft design. The materials could allow an aircraft to morph, or change shape, in the air. This technology could change aviation forever. Morphing technology would allow an aircraft to change into a form that makes them supersonic, and then back to another that is better suited to slow flight for landing. A morphing plane might also be able to repair itself.

ROBOT FLY SPIES

Back in World War I, fighters were developed to shoot down observation planes. Observation planes of the future could be very difficult to see. A number of robot spy planes are being developed to look like insects. Some are as small as a house fly. If flown in great numbers, they would be impossible to shoot down by missile armed fighters.

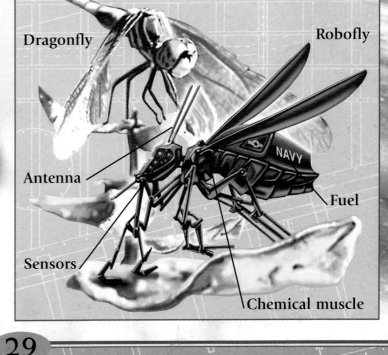

Dragonfly

Robofly

Antenna

Sensors

Fuel

Chemical muscle

SPOTTERS' GUIDE

Combat aircraft have changed dramatically from the wood and canvas Voisin 3 of World War I to the supersonic afterburning F-18 which first flew in 1978. Only about 60 years separate these two very different aircraft. There have been many great advances in technology. The Bf 110 had airborne radar with several nose mounted antennas, then called Christmas trees. Modern radar systems are so small they sit inside the nose cones of jets.

VOISIN 3
Country: France
Description: two seat fighter/reconnaissance
Length: 30 ft 8 in (9.4 m)
Wingspan: 53 ft (16.1 m)
Speed: 66 mph (106 km/h)

LOCKHEED P-38 LIGHTNING
Country: USA
Description: single seat long-range fighter
Length: 37 ft 10 in (11.5 m)
Wingspan: 52 ft (15.8 m)
Speed: 414 mph (665 km/h)

MESSERSCHMITT BF 110
Country: Germany
Description: two seat day and night fighter
Length: 39 ft 6 in (12 m)
Wingspan: 53 ft 3 in (16.2 m)
Speed: 317 mph (510 km/h)

DORNIER DO 215
Country: Germany
Description: four seat medium bomber and reconnaissance
Length: 51 ft 9 in (15.8 m)
Wingspan: 59 ft (18 m)
Speed: 280 mph (450 km/h)

F-89 SCORPION

Country: USA
Description: two seat all-weather interceptor
Length: 53 ft 8 in (16.5 m)
Wingspan: 59 ft 10 in (18.4 m)
Speed: 627 mph (1,000 km/h)

MC DONNELL DOUGLAS F-4 PHANTOM IID

Country: USA
Description: two seat carrier/land based multi-role fighter
Length: 63 ft (19.2 m)
Wingspan: 38 ft 4 in (11.7 m)
Speed: 1,006 mph (1,619 km/h)

GENERAL DYNAMICS F-16 FIGHTING FALCON

Country: USA
Description: single seat multi-role fighter
Length: 47 ft 7 in (14.5 m)
Wingspan: 31 ft (9.4 m)
Speed: 1,333 mph (2,145 km/h)

MC DONNELL DOUGLAS F-18 HORNET

Country: USA
Description: single seat carrier based fighter
Length: 56 ft (17 m)
Wingspan: 37 ft 6 in (11.4 m)
Speed: 1,190 mph (1,915 km/h)

INDEX

GLOSSARY

ALLIED Joined in an alliance or agreement to help each other. The Allies during World War II included Britain, France, the U.S.A., and the U.S.S.R.

COLD WAR A state of political tension and military rivalry that existed mainly between the United States and the Soviet Union from the end of World War II until the early 1990s.

COMMUNIST A government system where the state plans and controls the economy and owns all of its natural resources.

CONQUER To take over another country using force.

FALKLANDS WAR A war between Great Britain and Argentina in 1982 over a group of islands in the Atlantic ocean off the coast of Argentina.

FRONT The most forward line of a combat force.

INTERCEPTOR A fast-climbing, highly maneuverable fighter plane designed to stop the progress of enemy aircraft or missiles.

KOREAN WAR A war from 1950 to 1953 between North Korea aided by China, and South Korea aided by United Nations forces, mostly U.S. troops.

NASA The National Aeronautics and Space Administration, the American organization responsible for space flight and exploration.

NUCLEAR WEAPONS Very powerful and destructive weapons.

RADAR Short form for Radio Detecting and Ranging, a method of detecting objects such as enemy aircraft using radio waves reflected from their surfaces.

RETRACTABLE Something that can be drawn back.

SUPERSONIC Faster than the speed of sound.

SOVIET UNION The Union of Soviet Socialist Republics, a group of countries under communist rule from 1922–1991.

TRENCHES Deep ditches dug into the ground during warfare.

VIETNAM WAR A war from 1963 to 1975 between North Vietnam aided by China and the Soviet Union, and South Vietnam aided by the United States.

WESTERN NATIONS A term that refers to the non-communist countries of western Europe and North America.

WORLD WAR I A war fought from 1914 to 1918 in which Great Britain, France, Russia, Canada, the U.S.A. and other allies defeated Germany and Austria.

WORLD WAR II A war fought from 1939 to 1945 in which Great Britain, France, the Soviet Union, the U.SA., and other allies defeated Germany, Italy, and Japan.